S0-AHB-144

EN
construcción
Construction
SITE

LOS MONTACARGAS
FORKLIFTS

Dan Osier

Traducción al español: Eida de la Vega

PowerKiDS
press.

New York

Published in 2014 by The Rosen Publishing Group, Inc.
29 East 21st Street, New York, NY 10010

First Edition

Editor: Amelie von Zumbusch
Book Design: Andrew Povolny
Photo Research: Katie Stryker

Traducción al español: Eida de la Vega

Photo Credits: Cover, p. 15 iStockphoto/Thinkstock; p. 5 Thomas Barwick/Stone/Getty Images; p. 7 ekipaj/Shutterstock.com; p. 9 Rich Legg/E+/Getty Images; p. 11 Sorbis/Shutterstock.com; p. 13 Lloyd Paulson/Shutterstock.com; p. 17 nikshor/Shutterstock.com; p. 19 ndoeljindoel/Shutterstock.com; p. 21 George Doyle/Stockbyte/Thinkstock; p. 23 Michael Westhoff/E+/Getty Images.

Library of Congress Cataloging-in-Publication Data

Osier, Dan, author.
 Forklifts = Los montacargas / by Dan Osier ; translated by Eida de la Vega. — First edition.
     pages cm. — (Construction site = En construcción)
 English and Spanish.
 Includes index.
 ISBN 978-1-4777-3295-3 (library)
 1. Forklift trucks—Juvenile literature. 2. Construction equipment—Juvenile literature. I. Vega, Eida de la, translator. II. Osier, Dan. Forklifts. III. Osier, Dan. Forklifts. Spanish. IV. Title. V. Title: Montacargas. VI. Title: Fork lifts.
 TL296.O8518 2014
 621.8′63—dc23
                              2013022467

Websites: Due to the changing nature of Internet links, PowerKids Press has developed an online list of websites related to the subject of this book. This site is updated regularly. Please use this link to access the list: www.powerkidslinks.com/cs/forkli/

Manufactured in the United States of America

CPSIA Compliance Information: W14PK3 **For Further Information contact Rosen Publishing, New York, New York at 1-800-237-9932**

Contenido

Contents

¡Los **montacargas** son geniales! Pueden levantar grandes cargas.

Forklifts are cool! They can lift big loads.

Los puedes ver en sitios de construcción.

_____

You can see them at building sites.

También los puedes ver
en almacenes.

You can see them in
warehouses, too.

9

Algunos montacargas tienen **contrapesos** en la parte de atrás para evitar volcarse.

Some forklifts have **counterweights** at the back. These help them not tip over.

Los montacargas telescópicos tienen **brazos** que pueden alargarse. Eso les permite levantar cargas muy alto.

Telescopic forklifts have **booms**. Their booms can stretch out. This lets them lift loads very high.

13

Las compañías de montacargas más grandes están en Japón, Alemania y los Estados Unidos.

The biggest forklift companies are in Japan, Germany, and the United States.

La compañía Yale hizo
los primeros camiones
montacargas.

The Yale company made the
first forklift trucks.

17

Se requiere destreza para conducir un montacargas.

It takes skill to drive a forklift.

Y debes tener al menos
18 años.

You also must be at least 18
years old.

21

¿Te gustaría manejar
un montacargas
cuando crezcas?

_____

Would you like to drive a
forklift when you grow up?

HOW AM I DRIVING?

23

PALABRAS QUE DEBES SABER / WORDS TO KNOW

(el) brazo

boom

(el) contrapeso

counterweight

(el) montacargas

forklift

ÍNDICE

INDEX